THE TELLER REVIEW OF BOOKS
Vol. I Christianity, Culture & the State

THE TELLER REVIEW OF BOOKS

Vol. I Christianity, Culture & the State

Nadine L. Jackson, Editor-in-Chief

THE TELLER REVIEW OF BOOKS
Vol. I Christianity, Culture & the State

Nadine L. Jackson, Editor-in-Chief

Copyright © 2009-16 by TellerBooks™. All rights reserved. No part of this publication may be reproduced or transmitted in any form or by any means, including photocopying, recording, or copying to any storage and retrieval system, without express written permission from the copyright holder.

ISBN (13) (paperback): 978-1-68109-062-7
ISBN (10) (paperback): 1-68109-062-7
ISBN (13) (ePub): 978-1-68109-063-4
ISBN (10) (ePub): 1-68109-063-5

www.TellerBooks.com

THE TELLER REVIEW OF BOOKS™
Nadine L. Jackson, Editor-in-Chief

The Teller Review of Books™ (Editor-in-Chief: Nadine L. Jackson) provides succinct overviews and critical reviews of the seminal books shaping contemporary culture in the areas of law, faith, society and public policy. Milestones in political, cultural and religious thought, whether contemporary publications or the classics, form part of the corpus of reviewed works.

Each Volume of the Teller Review of Books™ consists of concise reviews of books that follow specific themes, including: Christianity, Culture & the State; Political Science and Public Policy; and Natural Law Thinking.

Table of Contents

TABLE OF CONTENTS 7
I.   MERE CHRISTIANITY (C. S. LEWIS) 9
     A.   The Case for Absolute Values 9
     B.   The Case for Christ 9
     C.   On Christian Living 10
II. A PRACTICAL VIEW OF CHRISTIANITY (WILLIAM WILBERFORCE) 13
     A.   Introduction 13
     B.   Review 13
     C.   Critique 15
III. SEPARATION OF CHURCH AND STATE (PHILIP HAMBURGER) 17
IV. ON TWO WINGS (MICHAEL NOVAK) 19
V.   NOTES TOWARDS A DEFINITION OF CULTURE (T.S. ELIOT) 21
VI. THE CHILDREN OF LIGHT AND THE CHILDREN OF DARKNESS (REINHOLD NIEBUHR) 23
VII. LECTURES ON CALVINISM (ABRAHAM KUYPER) 25
VIII. ABRAHAM KUYPER: A CENTENNIAL READER (JAMES D. BRATT, ED.) 29
     A.   Abraham Kuyper: His World and Work 29
     B.   Common Grace (1902-4) 29
     C.   Maranatha (1891) 30
     D.   Sphere Sovereignty (1880) 30
IX. CATHOLIC SOCIAL THOUGHT (DAVID J. O'BRIEN AND THOMAS A. SHANNON) 31
     A.   Rerum Novarum: The Condition of Labor (Leo XIII, 1891) 31
     B.   Quadragesimo Anno: After Forty Years (Pius XI, 1931) 32
     C.   Centesimus Annus: On the Hundredth Anniversary of Rerum Novarum (1991) 33
X.   COVENANT & POLITY IN BIBLICAL ISRAEL (DANIEL J. ELAZAR) 35
     A.   The Covenant Idea in the Bible and Politics 35
     B.   The Torah as Ancient Israel's Constitution 36
     C.   A Biblical Republic? 37
     D.   A Biblical Constitutional Monarchy? 38
     E.   Conclusion 39
XI. THE NAKED PUBLIC SQUARE (RICHARD JOHN NEUHAUS) 41
XII. A WORLD WITHOUT TYRANNY (DEAN C. CURRY) 43

	A.	Overview	43
	B.	Flaws	43
XIII.	CREATION REGAINED (ALBERT M. WOLTERS)		49
	A.	Introduction to the Christian Worldview	49
	B.	Creation, Fall, Redemption	49
	C.	Structure and Direction	50
XIV.	IN THE BEGINNING: FOUNDATIONS OF CREATION THEOLOGY (HERMAN BAVINCK)		51
	A.	Creation: God as Maker of Heaven and Earth	51
	B.	Man's Origins	52
	C.	Human Nature	52
	D.	Man's Destiny	52
	E.	Providence: God's Preservation of the Earth	53
	F.	Conclusion	54
XV.	THE LAST THINGS (HERMAN BAVINCK)		55
	A.	Review	55
	B.	Critique	56

I. Mere Christianity (C. S. Lewis)

2001 Harper San Francisco edition co-published by Zondervan, with a foreword by Kathleen Norris
"Clear, lucid, persuasive"

In this volume, C.S. Lewis, one of the most influential writers of the twentieth century, successfully lays out those basic tenets that nearly all Christians have held together at all times. He employs convincing arguments in plain language to point to a system of absolute truth and he then comes full circle by arguing that this system is fully realized in a Christian worldview.

A. The Case for Absolute Values

He opens the book by arguing that people hold to common perceptions of right and wrong, as can be evidenced in everyday, mundane situations. The statements that are exchanged in arguments, such as "That's my seat, I was there first" or "Come on, you promised," demonstrate this tendency (p. 3). People quarreling typically do not discard the standard against which their conduct is being measured; rather, they try to justify themselves according to the standard. This, says Lewis, points to a system of absolute values that people hold in common.

B. The Case for Christ

Lewis then challenges the reader to concede that he (the reader) has at some time or another violated the very standards of behavior that "we expect from other people" (p. 7). Thus, although people believe in transcendent standards, they have throughout history and throughout cultures typically not acted in accordance with these standards. This is the gateway through which Lewis sets up the argument that he will employ throughout the rest of the book: people need to be justified, and Christianity offers the answers in Christ.

The reader is challenged to examine the claims of Christ and to determine for himself whether or not Christ was God, as he claimed to be. If he was not, then he "would either be a lunatic--on a level with the man who says he is a poached egg--or else he would be the Devil of Hell" (p. 52). Lewis leaves no room for the view that Jesus was no more than a "great moral teacher", since no great moral teacher would claim to be God if he was merely man.

C. On Christian Living

After setting out the case for Christianity, Lewis discusses various aspects of Christian doctrine and behavior. The purpose and end of Christians is to become like "little Christs" while working out their salvation. Lewis discusses a series of relevant questions, including social morality, sexual morality, charity, hope, faith, and the difficulty of Christian living.

Of the latter sections of the book, one of Lewis's strongest is chapter 6 of book 3, where he discusses the idea of Christian marriage. He makes the case for the leadership of the man in Christian marriage in a way that is strikingly relevant. He begins from the premise that there needs to be a leader in the relationship and, based on the natural differences between men and women, as well as some anecdotes and arguments based on intuition and some common sense, Lewis states why the leadership of the man, as taught in the Scriptures, is in keeping with human nature. My only criticism to this chapter is that Lewis starts on the premise that disagreement will naturally arise, and because there can be no democracy in a relationship of two, either the man or the wife needs to take the lead. The problem with this is that it ignores the place of leadership even in the absence of disagreement. For example, Adam was Eve's head in prelapsarian Eden, where there was neither sin nor conflict.

Lewis also discusses the two aspects of love that married couples will experience, the first being the "falling in love" and the second being the "staying in love" that should last for the rest of their lives. He writes that "What we call 'being in love' is a glorious state, and, in several ways, good for us. It helps to make us generous and courageous, it opens our eyes not only to the beauty of the beloved but to all beauty, and it subordinates (especially at first) our merely animal sexuality; in that sense, love is the great conqueror of lust. No one in his senses would deny that being in love is far better than either common sensuality or cold self-centeredness. But, as I said before, 'the most dangerous thing you can do is to take any one impulse of our own nature and set it up as the thing you ought to follow at all costs'. Being in love is a good thing, but it is not the best thing. There are many things below it, but there are also things above it. You cannot make it the basis of a whole life. It is a noble feeling, but it is still a felling. Now no feeling can be relied on to last in its full intensity, or even to last at all. Knowledge can last, principles can last, habits can last; but feelings come and go. And in fact, whatever people say, the state called 'being in love' usually does not last. If the old fairy-tale ending

'They lived happily ever after' is taken to mean 'They felt for the next fifty years exactly as they felt the day before they were married', then it says what probably never was nor ever would be true, and would be highly undesirable if it were. Who could bear to live in that excitement for even five years? What would become of your work, your appetite, your sleep, your friendships? But, of course, ceasing to be 'in love' need not mean ceasing to love. Love in this second sense--love as distinct from 'being in love'--is not merely a feeling. It is a deep unity, maintained by the will and deliberately strengthened by habit; reinforced by (in Christian marriages) the grace which both partners ask, and receive, from God. They can have this love for each other even at those moments when they do not like each other; as you love yourself even when you do not like yourself. They can retain this love even when each would easily, if they allowed themselves, be 'in love' with someone else. 'Being in love' first moved them to promise fidelity: this quieter love enables them to keep the promise. It is on this love that the engine of marriage is run: being in love was the explosion that started it" (p. 108-109). Lewis speaks with remarkable clarity and wisdom for a man who, at the time he wrote the passage, was unmarried.

II. A Practical View of Christianity (William Wilberforce)

A. Introduction

William Wilberforce (1759 - 1833) was a member of the English Parliament for the County of York who dedicated his life to abolishing the slave trade. He once wrote that "Almighty God has set before me two great objectives, the abolition of the slave trade and the reformation of manners." This great burden laid on his heart throughout his life, and gave him little leave for rest. He believed that the two were related, for without the reformation of manners through addressing cultural malaise, it would be nearly impossible to abolish the slave trade.

It was within this context that Wilberforce wrote *A Practical View of Christianity* (originally titled *A Practical View of the Prevailing Religious System of Professed Christians, in the Middle and Higher Classes in this Country, Contrasted with Real Christianity*). He hoped to challenge the nominal Christianity of the middle and upper classes of England and to inspire the nation with a fresh view of a religion whose goal was not empty ritual, but transformation through Christ. The book sent a shockwave throughout the nation and has been credited with helping to start the second Great Awakening of England.

Wilberforce was a saint in every sense of the word. He restlessly fought for the abolition of the slave trade, presenting motion after motion for abolition, each in turn being thrown out by Parliament, until at last in 1807, Wilberforce's bill passed. Yet he did not stop with the abolition of the slave trade. Wilberforce dedicated nearly two decades thereafter to securing the complete emancipation of the slaves in England. With a circle of trusted friends known as the "Clapham Circle," Wilberforce proved how a small group can change history.

That so recent a saint left to posterity a fine piece of literature that both warns us of religious nominalism and inspires us to greater depths of God-honoring conducts proves how blessed we have been by Wilberforce. We have not only his legacy of freeing the slaves, but we also have his words passed down to us with the same crispness and relevance that they had two hundred years ago. The entire book is riddled with so many scriptural citations that one cannot doubt that Wilberforce had the heart of a man who loved and sought to honor God.

B. Review

Wilberforce sets out to trace the "chief defects of the religious system of the bulk of professed Christians" in England. He points out that "their low idea of the importance of Christianity in general, their inadequate conceptions of all its leading doctrines, and the effect hereby naturally produced in relaxing the strictness of its practical system." He distinguishes these "nominal" believers from "true" believers, stating that the Christianity of the nominal believers "*is not Christianity.*"

Wilberforce does not set out to "vindicate the Divine origin" of Christianity, but he continually touts the Christian faith, for whenever it has at all prevailed, Christianity "has raised the general standard of morals to a height before unknown" (p. 209). True Christianity transforms communities and individuals, but the England of his day had largely lost this true Christianity. English Christians were no longer interested in the truths of Christ, but rather, sought religious nominalism. It is no wonder that such a society was able to call itself "Christian" on the one hand while condoning slavery on the other hand.

The bulk of professed English Christians do not truly understand what Christianity means. Their understanding is at best superficial; Christianity to them is like other religions or like a mere set of moral principles. This becomes plain when we "[v]iew their plan of life and their ordinary conduct." It becomes difficult to discriminate "between them and professed unbelievers."

Nominal Christianity has arisen because professed Christians have failed to take scriptural teachings seriously. They overlook or deny, for example, the biblical reality of man's fallenness and corruption. Wilberforce exclaims of man: "How is his reason clouded, his affections perverted; his conscience stupified! How do anger, and envy, and hatred, and revenge, spring up in his wretched bosom! How is he a slave to the meanest of his appetites! What fatal propensities does he discover to evil! What inaptitude to good!" Yet then-contemporary Christians refused to believe this, thus depriving themselves of life in the Scriptures and in Christ. "What lively emotions are [the Scriptures] calculated to excite in us of self-abasement, and abhorrence of our sins; and of humble hope, and firm faith, and heavenly joy, and ardent love, and active unceasing gratitude!"

Wilberforce further comments that "They who hold the fundamental doctrines of Scripture in their due force, hold also in its due degree of purity the practical system which Scripture inculcates." Yet he goes on to accuse nominal Christians: "But they who explain away [the fundamental doctrines of Scripture], soften down [purity of living] also, and reduce it to the level of their own defective scheme." This second group lowers the moral standards demanded of all Christians in the Scriptures.

Wilberforce closes with a call to all Christians to "strive in all things to recommend their profession, and to put to silence the vain scoffs of ignorant objectors. Let them boldly assert the cause of Christ in an age when so many, who bear the name of Christians, are ashamed of Him: and let them consider as devolved on them the important duty of suspending for a while the fall of their country, and, perhaps, of performing a still more extensive service to society at large; not by busy interference in politics, in which it cannot but be confessed there is much uncertainty; but rather by that sure and radical benefit of restoring the influence of Religion, and of raising the standard of morality." Let true Christians be furthermore "active, useful, generous towards others; manifestly moderate and self-denying in themselves. Let them be ashamed of idleness, as they would be of the most acknowledged sin."

C. Critique

Wilberforce's bold work is a splash of cold water on complacent Christians of his day. One may argue that the siren that Wilberforce sounds is one of judgment, yet judgment cannot be avoided when a nation that calls itself Christian degraded basic human dignity through cruel institutions such as slavery. Confronting a country that completely compromised the Gospels and the credibility of Christianity, Wilberforce called his nation to higher principles and finally realized his dreams when through his tireless efforts, slavery was abolished from England forever.

III. Separation of Church and State (Philip Hamburger)

"A clear, concise, and well-researched history of the Establishment Clause"

Constitutional legal scholar Philip Hamburger, formerly a professor of law at the University of Chicago and currently professor of law at Columbia Law School, argues in "Separation of Church and State" that America's modern conception of the First Amendment's Establishment Clause has failed to make an adequate distinction between the establishment of religion, which the founders intended to prohibit, and the "separation of church and state," a later development that was almost never cited by eighteenth century Americans. Hamburger offers both academic and non-academic readers alike a thoroughly researched and engaging presentation of the history of the Establishment Clause and how it came to be misapplied to the detriment of religion in the American public square.

How did the nation depart from a Constitution that guaranteed religious liberty to erect a "wall of separation between church and state"? Hamburger traces the problem to Thomas Jefferson, who in 1802 in his Letter to the Danbury Baptist Association reflected on "that act of the whole American people which declared that their legislature should 'make no law respecting an establishment of religion, or prohibiting the free exercise thereof,' thus building a wall of separation between Church & State.'" Jefferson's phrase would later be adopted by the Supreme Court. Justice Black, writing for the majority of the Supreme Court in Everson v. Board of Education of Ewing (1947), adopted Jefferson's separation of church and state and made it "the foundation of subsequent establishment clause jurisprudence." Five years later, Justice Douglas in Zorach v. Clauson (1952), affirmed Black's basic principle but expressed concern over the extent to which its implications could be taken. Although the separation of church and state must be complete, the First Amendment did "not say that in every and all respects there shall be a separation of Church and State," for if this were the case, municipalities would even be prohibited from providing police services to churches or other religious groups.

Yet things would soon change. Within the context of private, religious schools, Chief Justice Burger writing for the majority in Lemon v. Kurtzman (1971), held that statutes could only provide funding for religious schools when the following elements were met: "First, the statute must have a secular legislative purpose; second, its principal or primary effect must be one that neither advances nor inhibits religion ... finally, the statute must not foster 'an excessive government entanglement with religion.'" Applying these elements, the Court struck down Pennsylvania and Rhode Island statutes that provided aid to non-public schools, including church-related schools. The court would go further, excluding religion in public schools in Wallace v. Jaffree (1985) (Stevens, J.), nativity scenes in Allegheny County v. Greater Pittsburgh ACLU (1989) (Blackmun, J.), and prayer at a graduation ceremony in Lee v. Weisman (1992) (Kennedy, J.). Throughout this chaos, the dissents of Justices Rehnquist and Scalia often fell on deaf ears. As Rehnquist articulated in Wallace, the separation standard lacked historical support and "proved all but useless as a guide to sound constitutional adjudication."

Hamburger concludes by highlighting the fact that the original opponents of the government establishment of religion did not demand a complete separation between church and state; although they opposed governmental financial benefits to established churches, they typically did not reject the conventional view that "there was a necessary and valuable moral connection between religion and government." Today, however, the opponents of establishment have taken us to a different place, where the mere hint of government endorsement of religion is viewed as contrary to the constitution. The nation thus finds itself in a place where the very religious liberty that the U.S. Constitution was designed to protect has instead become undermined.

IV. On Two Wings (Michael Novak)

"An Effective Defense of the Importance of Religious Faith in the American Founding"

Michael Novak's *On Two Wings* sets out to correct the way the story of the American founding has been told in recent times. Although both reason and religious faith were essential wings to the American founding, the recounting of the story has cut off faith from the founding, focusing only on the secular philosophy of the Enlightenment in explaining the story. Michael Novak, bringing to the reader dozens of firsthand accounts of the writings of the founders, sets out to prove that the founders believed that they were acting on a religious duty in establishing a new model of self-government.

Novak provides the reader with an arsenal of quotes and writings of the founders to support his thesis. George Washington, for example, after escaping what many believed would be a catastrophic battle in August of 1776 against the Royal Army in Long Island, wrote to Samuel Langdon that "The man must be bad indeed who can look upon the events of the American Revolution without feeling the warmest gratitude towards the great Author of the Universe whose divine interposition was frequently manifested in our behalf" (p. 191). Of the 3,154 citations in the writings of the founders, "nearly 1,100 references (34 percent) are to the Bible" (p. 6). Invocations of the name of God and prayers of thanksgiving to Him are frequent among the founders. Considering the fact that the first act of the Continental Congress was an act of public prayer and that the Declaration of Independence invokes God four times--as Lawgiver, Creator, Judge, and Providence--Novak concludes that "what the founding generation did cannot be explained by the Enlightenment alone" (p. 24).

The other wing of the American founding--common sense--enabled the founders to reason plainly and to reflect soberly on the conditions of man. This common sense went hand in hand with religious faith. Even Thomas Paine, the author of *Common Sense*, was so opposed to atheism that he sailed to France to fight against it after 1789. Virtually all the founders believed not in a watered down form of religion, but rather, held religious faith in the Judeo-Christian tradition. Judaism and Christianity "reinforced in men's minds the role of reason in human affairs, as well as the idea of a cosmos open to liberty" (p. 46).

Interestingly, Novak describes John Locke as one of the most influential political thinkers in inspiring the founders. Of the political theorists who were cited in the writings of the founders, only Montesquieu and Blackstone eclipsed Locke: "In a total of 3,154 citations, Montesquieu was cited most (8.3 percent), followed closely by Blackstone (7.9 percent), third Locke (2.9)" (p. 183). Novak writes "if any in the founding generation felt incompatibility between Locke and the Protestant tradition (as many writers do today), they did not mention it; and many preachers and writers cited both Locke and the Bible in the same paragraph" (p. 6).

Novak follows his study with an appendix providing summaries of the many signers of the Declaration of Independence and of the Constitution such as Robert Sherman, Benjamin Rush, and George Mason, who, though they are not as well-known as Jefferson, Franklin, Madison, or some of the more "secular" of the founders, were important leaders in their generation and held strong religious beliefs. He recounts, for example, Alexander Hamilton's "tender requests that the Holy Eucharist might be brought to him on his death bed" (p. 150).

The book is generally effective at dissipating the myths on the secular nature of America's founding. Yet Novak's statements are not always supported by the evidence he provides. He writes, for example, that "Virtually all the founders of the American Republic believed mightily that of all philosophies and religions, the Jewish and Christian religion is the best foundation for republican institutions" (p. 33). He then quotes James Madison, Thomas Jefferson, and other founders, yet the quotes offered do not even mention Judaism or Christianity or their importance to the founders. For example, Jefferson wrote: "And can the liberties of a nation be thought secure when we have removed their only firm basis, a conviction in the minds of the people that these liberties are the gift of God?" (p. 33). The "God" that Jefferson refers to is not necessarily the God of the Christian faith, but rather, may be the God of any religious faith that upholds the supernatural.

V. Notes Towards a Definition of Culture (T.S. Eliot)

"An abstruse essay that sheds some light on an abstruse subject matter"

Eliot begins by conceding that the subject of his study "involves the risk of error at every moment" and is "so difficult that I am not sure I grasp it myself except in flashes, or that I comprehend all its implications." He defines culture as "not merely the sum of several activities, but a way of life" of people living together in one place. It is "made visible in their arts, in their social system, in their habits and customs, in their religion." He warns the reader about the danger of committing two errors: "that of regarding religion and culture as separate things between which there is a relation and that of identifying [equating] religion and culture." Culture and religion are separate and distinct, but they are intricately interwoven.

Eliot breaks culture down into three classes: the individual, the group, and whole society. The culture of the individual is "dependent upon the culture of a group or class, and that the culture of the group or class is dependent upon the culture of the whole society to which that group or class belongs." He begins his study with culture at the whole society level, setting out to avoid.

The material organization of a nation is inextricably linked with its spiritual life. In the context of Europe, if the spiritual organization dies, "then what you will organize will not be Europe, but merely a mass of human beings speaking several different languages." "In the most primitive societies no clear distinction is visible between religious and non-religious activities; and that as we proceed to examine the more developed societies, we perceive a greater distinction, and finally contrast and opposition, between these activities."

The culture of the West has been formed through common conceptions that have been handed down from the ancient civilizations of Greece, Rome, and Israel. These legacies have given way to common conceptions of private and public morality, a conception of Roman law, and common standards of art and literature. It is the duty of men of letters throughout Europe to pass on this culture, unadulterated by political motives, to future generations by producing "those excellent works which mark a superior civilization."

VI. The Children of Light and the Children of Darkness (Reinhold Niebuhr)

"Important Insights on Democracy"

Reinhold Niebuhr's *Children of Light and Children of Darkness* brings to the discussion on democracy many needed insights on human nature that have been articulated by Calvin, Augustine, and a host of other Church Fathers. Although the insights presented in the book are not particularly novel or original, they remind modern society, which tends to cast a great deal of faith in government, of man's sinful propensities and how this should limit what we are to expect of democracy and of government more generally.

In his book, Niebuhr argues that "a free society prospers best in a cultural, religious and moral atmosphere which encourages neither a too pessimistic nor too optimistic view of human nature" (p. viii), and that this atmosphere is best served in democracy. "Man's capacity for justice makes democracy possible, but man's inclination to injustice makes democracy necessary" (p. xiii).

Niebuhr designates the moral cynics as the "children of this world" or "children of darkness" (p. 9), making a reference to Luke 16:8: "the sons of this world are more shrewd in their generation than the sons of light." He defines the "children of light" as those who believe that "self-interest should be brought under the discipline of a higher law" (p. 9) and "in harmony with a more universal good" (p. 10). The children of darkness, in contrast, "know no law beyond the self" and they are wise because they "understand the power of self-interest" (p. 10). The children of light are foolish because they have a naïve, sentimental view of human nature that does not recognize the perils of anarchy.

The error of modern culture is pinned on a rejection of the doctrine of original sin and thus the neglect of the fact that there is "some corruption of inordinate self love" in all human moral or social achievements (p. 17). If this crucial truth is denied or ignored, democratic civilization will not survive. "The children of light must be armed with the wisdom of the children of darkness but remain free from their malice" (p. 41).

On the question of individualism, Niebuhr asserts that man is by nature a social being called to live in community. At the same time, he is an individual and "[t]he 'I' is so intimately related to the 'mine' and the 'thou' and the 'thine' that relations of accord or conflict between individuals usually imply questions of property" (p. 86). Property, Niebuhr asserts, is by its nature intended to be privately held in man's postlapsarian state, for after the fall of man, "communism became impossible" (p. 93-4). Pope Leo XIII recognized this when he wrote in his encyclical *Rerum Novarum* that the principle of private property is "pre-eminently in conformity with human nature" (p. 93). Yet the bourgeoisie has committed two errors with respect to property: (i) the "excessive individualism of the bourgeois property concept, which is part and parcel of a general exaggeration of individual free in middle-class existence"; and (ii) the "prevailing presupposition of liberal thought that property represents primarily an ordinate and defensive power to be used against the inclination of others to take advantage of the self" (p. 98-9). Marxism has avoided this error, only to commit another: it has fallen into an illusion by failing to recognize the potential of socialized property to be used as an instrument of particular interest against the general interest.

As G. K. Chesterton has said, "Tolerance is the virtue of people who do not believe anything" (p. 130). Yet one of the great errors of modern children of light is that by opening the public square to all opinions, all religious convictions will gradually dissipate, leaving "an essential uniformity through the common conviction of 'men of good-will' who have been enlightened by modern liberal education" (p. 131). This ultimately moves towards either a secular covert religion or a relativism that acknowledges the finiteness of human knowledge. Rather, to save civilization from either secularism or authoritarianism, the religious groups of a community must be capable of humility and charity (p. 137-8). As Niebuhr affirms, "Democratic life requires a spirit of tolerant cooperation between individuals and groups which can be achieved by neither moral cynics, who know no law beyond their own interest, nor by moral idealists, who acknowledge such a law but are unconscious of the corruption which insinuates itself into the statement of it by even the most disinterested idealists" (p. 152).

VII. Lectures on Calvinism (Abraham Kuyper)

"Important Reading for Christians in Government and Politics"

This is a book that is important for Christians going into government and politics. Abraham Kuyper (1837 - 1920), a Dutch politician, journalist, theologian, and former prime minister of the Netherlands, explains how the Christian faith should inform all aspects of the Christian's life and worldview, and how it should infuse religion, politics, science, and art. My review will mainly explore Kuyper's treatment of politics, since I consider it to be the most important in the book, but I will touch up on some other chapters as well.

The Dutch theologian and philosopher Abraham Kuyper served as prime minister of the Netherlands from 1901 to 1905. In 1870, he became Editor-in-chief of the daily newspaper *The Standard* and he would later become the editor of *The Herald*, a Christian weekly paper. In 1874, he was elected to the lower house of Parliament, where he served until 1877, and in 1880, he founded the Free University of Amsterdam, which takes the Bible as the unconditional basis for the structuring of human knowledge.

Dr. Kuyper has said that "One desire has been the ruling passion of my life. One high motive has acted like a spur upon my mind and soul ... It is this: That in spite of all worldly opposition, God's holy ordinances shall be established again in the home, in the school and in the State for the good of the people" (p. iii). Throughout all of his writings, Kuyper seeks to establish Christ as "King in every department of human life and activity" (p. vi).

According to Kuyper, there are three sources of authority under God: Church, the State, and the family. Under his theory of "sphere sovereignty," each of these holds its own sphere of influence and may not transgress its boundaries. For instance, the State may not impose its laws in the independent sovereign "social sphere," the "corporative sphere of universities, guilds, associations, etc.," the "domestic sphere of the family and of married life," and the "communal autonomy" (p. 96). Within these independent spheres, Government may only "compel mutual regard for the boundary-lines of each," "defend individuals and the weak ones" in those spheres, and coerce all to bear the "financial burdens for the maintenance of the natural unity of the State" (p. 97).

Under Kuyper's political system, the State may not interfere with the sovereignty of the Church in weeding out heterodoxy from orthodoxy. Kuyper thereby rejects Calvin's demand for the "intervention of the government in the matter of religion" (p. 99). The State cannot "form an individual judgment, as to which of those many Churches is the true one" (p. 105). Only "the system of a free Church, in a free State, may be honored from a Calvinistic standpoint" (p. 106).

Kuyper lays out the basis for the State's God-given authority and need for constitutional limits of authority, which is similarly limited by God. "No man has the right to rule over another man" (p. 82), he writes. It is not in man's prelapsarian nature to submit to state authority. Had it not been for sin, there would be no need for government, which bears the sword to "mete out corporeal punishment to the criminal ..., to defend the honor and the rights and the interests of the State against its enemies ..., [and] to thwart at home all forcible rebellion" (p. 93). However, even in a prelapsarian state, submission in the family, in the Church, and before God would have continued. Without sin, "political life, in its entirety, would have evolved itself, after a patriarchal fashion, from the life of the family" (p. 80).

Kuyper goes on to discuss the popular sovereignty proclaimed in Paris in 1789 as well as state sovereignty, which had been spreading throughout Europe at the time. Because each of these theories rejects God--whereas State sovereignty puts the State above God, popular sovereignty puts the people and their free wills above God--Kuyper in turn rejects them. He contrasts these movements to the rebellion against Spain, under William the Silent, the English Glorious Revolution, which overthrew the Stuarts, and the American Revolution, all of which proceeded from an acknowledgement of God. He contrasts the American Revolution with the French Revolution. In the former, although the people were held to be above the government, God was viewed as above the people. Perhaps Hamilton captures this distinction best when he considered "the French Revolution to be no more akin to the American Revolution than the faithless wife in a French novel is like the Puritan matron in New England" (p. 87). The liberty in the French Revolution "for every Christian to agree with the unbelieving majority is in turn contrasted with the notion of liberty in Calvinism--"a liberty of conscience, which enables every man to serve God according to his own conviction and the dictates of his own heart" (p. 109).

Kuyper concludes by stating that the chief purpose of his lectures "was to eradicate the wrong idea that Calvinism represented an exclusively dogmatical and ecclesiastical movement. Calvinism did not stop at a church-order, but expanded in a life-system, and did not exhaust its energy in a dogmatical construction, but created a life- and world-view" (p. 171). He goes on to lay out the framework for a coalition between Protestants and Catholics to defend "those fundamentals of our Christian creed now most fiercely assaulted by the modern spirit" (p. 183). United with Rome on the fundamentals, Protestants can more effectively promote "the Bible as given by inspiration of God over against a purely human product; the Ten Commandments as ordained by God over against a mere archeological document; the ordinances of God absolutely established over against an ever-changing law and morality spun out of man's subjective consciousness" (p. 183), and the other doctrines key to the Christian worldview. "Therefore," he concludes, "let me ask if Romish theologians take up the sword to do valiant and skillful battle against the same tendency that we ourselves mean to fight to the death, is it not the part of wisdom to accept the valuable help of their elucidation?" (p. 184). In this way, he argues for a political coalition that would go on to hold sway against the revolutionary forces sweeping Europe at the time.

in a dogmatical construction, but created a life- and world-view" (p. 171). He goes on to lay out the framework for a coalition between Protestants and Catholics to defend "those fundamentals of our Christian creed now most fiercely assaulted by the modern spirit" (p. 183). United with Rome on the fundamentals, Protestants can more effectively promote "the Bible as given by inspiration of God over against a purely human product; the Ten Commandments as ordained by God over against a mere archeological document; the ordinances of God absolutely established over against an ever-changing law and morality spun out of man's subjective consciousness" (p. 183), and the other doctrines key to the Christian worldview. "Therefore," he concludes, "let me ask if Romish theologians take up the sword to do valiant and skillful battle against the same tendency that we ourselves mean to fight to the death, is it not the part of wisdom to accept the valuable help of their elucidation?" (p. 184). In this way, he argues for a political coalition that would go on to hold sway against the revolutionary forces sweeping Europe at the time.

VIII. Abraham Kuyper: A Centennial Reader (James D. Bratt, Ed.)

"Christ's complete sovereignty and total dominion"

A. Abraham Kuyper: His World and Work

Abraham Kuyper (1837 - 1920) was a Dutch politician, journalist, theologian, and prime minister of the Netherlands. His work can be characterized by an "insistence on a consistent logic rooted in first principles and carried out until it comprehended every domain in life" (p. 4). Calvinism was Kuyper's "soul and his system, the purest form of Christianity, the treasure of the past, the hope of the future" (p. 1). He was deeply suspicious of modernity and sought to elaborate a worldview that would imbue all of the areas of life with the Christian perspective.

B. Common Grace (1902-4)

Common grace is the hinge of Kuyper's constructive theology. His work on the Reform doctrine of common grace was far reaching, but his opponents "complained that this was more 'invention' than elaboration" (p. 165). The distinction between saving grace and common grace is "evident from the undeniable fact that, without common grace, the elect would not have been born, would not have seen the light of day" (p. 169). Not all common grace impacts all aspects of human life in the same way; one common grace "aims at the *interior*, another at the *exterior* part of our existence. The former is operative wherever civic virtue, a sense of domesticity, natural love, the practice of human virtue, the improvement of the public conscience, integrity, mutual loyalty among people, and a feeling for piety leaven life. The latter is in evidence when human power over nature increases, when invention upon invention enriches life, when international communication is improved, the arts flourish, the sciences increase our understanding ..." (p. 181).

Contrasting his view to the dialectic distinction between the church as institution and the church as organism, Kuyper proposes that the church is both. The church as institution is comprised of its baptized, believing members. It is like a circle whose circumference increases as its membership grows. Yet there is another circle whose circumference is determined "by the length of the ray that shines out from the church institute over the life of people and nation. Since this second circle ... is not circumscribed by a certain number of people listed in church directories, and does not have its own office bearers but is interwoven with the very fabric of national life, this extra-institutional influence at work in society points to the *church as organism*" (p. 195).

C. Maranatha (1891)

This was the keynote address at the Antirevolutionary Party Convention where "Kuyper's rhetorical prowess swept the 700-plus delegates" (p 206). The speech "Maranatha," which means "Our Lord, come!" or "Our Lord has come" in Aramaic, united the Antirevolutionary Party as Kuyper recited lines from Da Costa's "Forward in the name of the Lord" (p. 227). Kuyper calls for "*universal* proportional suffrage but on the basis of the *family*, for a restoration of the old guilds in a new form, for Chambers of Labor and Agriculture," and for a "*spirit of the Compassionate One* [to] be poured out over our whole government administration" (p. 225).

D. Sphere Sovereignty (1880)

This inaugural address at the Free University of Amsterdam represents the summa of Kuyper's thought. He lays out a framework for sphere sovereignty and for the State's role therein. He recognizes that "The various spheres of life cannot do without the State sphere, for just as one space can limit another, so one sphere can limit another unless the State fixes their boundaries by law" (p. 472).

Some twenty years later, Kuyper expanded on this thesis by discussing the scholarly realm: "scholarly research is not a matter of human pride but a God-given duty. The honor of God demands that the human mind penetrate the entire system of creation to discover His greatness and wisdom there and to translate these into human thought through human words" (p. 474). The scholarly realm must remain "Sovereign in its own sphere" and not "degenerate under the guardianship of Church or State" (p. 476). Kuyper upholds the University's scholarship as being "free," which he defines not as "detached from its principle," but rather, as that "everyone can freely build on the foundation of *his own* principles, in the style of *his own* method, with the cornice being the results of *his own* research" (p. 486).

Kuyper goes on to state, "Oh, no single piece of our mental world is to be hermetically sealed off from the rest, and there is not a square inch in the whole domain of our human existence over which Christ, who is Sovereign over all, does not cry: 'Mine!'"

IX. Catholic Social Thought (David J. O'Brien and Thomas A. Shannon)

"The classic texts of Catholic social teaching"

This volume offers readers the classic texts of Catholic social teaching, and the way that teaching has evolved in the last two centuries. Following is a review of some of the most influential writings discussed in the book.

A. *Rerum Novarum*: The Condition of Labor (Leo XIII, 1891)

Leo XIII (1810-1903) served as the two hundred fifty seventh pope from 1878 to 1903. He was an extraordinarily influential pope who was interested in the advancement of learning, opened the Vatican archives to all scholars, and founded the Catholic University of America in Washington, D.C. In 1891, at a time when capitalism and the industrial revolution were underway in transforming much of Europe, Leo wrote the great encyclical *Rerum Novarum* ("New Things") to all bishops of the Catholic Church. At the time, two classes had emerged in Europe: the industrialists, who enjoyed wealth and luxury, and the laborers, who were in general oppressed by poverty. In his encyclical, Leo XIII tried to convince Catholics to "concentrate less on politics and more on the 'social question'" in order to restore "order and authority" (p. 13).

Leo attempts to lay out a system of social action that would later be called "subsidiarity" by Pope Pius XI. Under this system, issues are dealt with by the most local level of administration, such as the family, household, or local community, and government or the State are only involved when issues cannot be effectively handled on a local level. Leo writes that the idea that civil government should at its own discretion "penetrate and pervade the family and the household, is a great and pernicious mistake" (p. 18, § 11). But if a family finds itself "in great difficulty, utterly friendless, and without prospect for help, it is right that extreme necessity be met by public aid" (p. 18-19, § 11). It is therefore natural and necessary that the State play some role in the work of remedy and relief by assuring that laws, institutions, and "the general character and administration of the commonwealth … produce of themselves public well-being and private prosperity" (p. 27, § 25).

Leo continues by analyzing the ideas animating socialism, such as the notion of "class warfare." He opposes this idea when he writes: "Just as the symmetry of the human body is the result of the disposition of the members of the body, so in a State it is ordained by nature that [employers and employees] should exist in harmony and agreement ... capital cannot do without labor nor labor without capital" (p. 20, § 15).

He further outlines a series of workmen's rights, including the right to strike (p. 29, § 31), to a day of rest of Sundays and on certain festivals (p. 29, § 32), to reasonable hours of labor (p. 30, § 33), and to a just wage (p. 31, § 34). Regarding the right to a just wage, Leo argues for a perspective that goes beyond a mere contract theory of work, for "there is a dictate of nature more imperious and more ancient than any bargain between man and man" (p. 31, § 34). An employer does not fulfill his duty by simply paying the worker an agreed-to wage, for it is not within the workman's right to even accept a wage when it is below the level necessary for the support of himself and of his family. Rather, every worker "has a right to procure what is required in order to live" (p. 31, § 34). When employers fail to honor this basic right, the State is to be appealed to for protection.

B. *Quadragesimo Anno*: After Forty Years (Pius XI, 1931)

Pius XI served from 1922 to 1939 as the two hundred sixtieth pope. In 1931, amidst worldwide unemployment and economic depression, Pius published the *Quadragesimo Anno* ("After Forty Years") to commemorate the *Rerum Novarum* on its fortieth anniversary and to offer insights into the encyclical's legacy and influence. As a result of the *Rerum Novarum*, writes Pius, civil rulers, more conscious of their obligations to "realize public well-being and private prosperity" (p. 47, § 25), at last "set their hearts and minds to the promotion of a broader social policy" (p. 47, § 26). The encyclical brought about a host of other reforms and encouraged and taught "Christian workingmen to form unions according to their several trades" (p. 48, § 31), thus preventing them from falling into the attractions of socialist organizations.

Regarding the principle of just distribution, writes Pius, a balanced middle ground must be sought after in order to prevent erroneous doctrines. Both the wealthy class that deems that the wealthy "should receive everything and the laborer nothing" as well as the propertyless class that "demand for themselves all the fruits of production" (p. 55, § 57) have stepped outside of the periphery of this balanced middle ground. It must always be recognized that the earth ministers "to the needs of all" (p. 55, § 56) and each class must accordingly "receive its due share" (p. 56, § 58). However, Pius denies the validity of the claim that the wage contract is essentially unjust and should be replaced with the contract of partnership; as Leo XIII so boldly made clear, both labor and capital are necessary in the harmony of business enterprise.

Drawing off of the ideas outlined in Leo's encyclical, Pius coins the term "subsidiarity" to refer to the principle outlined in the *Rerum Novarum* under which the State allows subordinate groups to handle matters and concerns of lesser importance that would otherwise dissipate the efforts of the State. This in turn allows the State to more effectively do all those things that belong to it alone, such as "directing, supervising, encouraging, [and] restraining" (p. 60, § 80). Pius highlights that "the more faithfully this principle of 'subsidiarity' is followed and a hierarchical order prevails among the various organizations, the more excellent will be the authority and efficiency of society, and the happier and more prosperous the condition of the commonwealth" (p. 60, § 80).

This principle is not new within Catholic social thought. Although the term is coined by Pius and the idea perhaps best expounded by Leo, it can be traced to Aquinas's discussions of private associations and beyond. Pius writes that the principle cannot be set aside or changed in social philosophy and remains "fixed and unchangeable" (p. 60, § 79).

C. *Centesimus Annus*: On the Hundredth Anniversary of Rerum Novarum (1991)

John Paul II served from 1978 to 2005 as the two hundred sixty fifth pope. In his encyclical *Centesimus Annus* ("After One Hundred Years"), a universal letter addressed to all Christians and "Men and Women of Good Will," John Paul II commemorated the one hundredth anniversary of the *Rerum Novarum* and echoed the calls of his predecessor Pope Leo XIII. The encyclical, coming at the heels of the 1989 fall of communism and the dissolution of the Soviet Union, celebrates the principles set forth in the *Rerum Novarum* and its warnings against unchecked socialism as well as impersonal capitalism, pointing instead to a third way that has come to be called "economic personalism," which is a form of compassionate or social market capitalism with human dignity at its center.

In *Centesimus Annus*, John Paul calls for trade unions, for example, to play a role in negotiating contracts and helping workers "share in a fully human way in the life of their place of employment." Moreover, he calls to the state to "contribute to the achievement" of this goal by, for example, "creating favorable conditions for the free exercise of economic activity" (p. 450-51, § 15).

Pope John Paul based his arguments largely on who man is anthropologically as created in God's image with transcendent dignity. For Pope John Paul II, Christian anthropology is "really a chapter of theology, and for this reason, the church's social doctrine, by its concern for man and by its interest in him and in the way he conducts himself in the world, 'belongs to the field ... of theology and particularly to moral theology'" (p. 480, § 55). John Paul writes that "Not only is it wrong from the ethical point of view to disregard human nature, which is made for freedom, but in practice it is impossible to do so. Where society is so organized as to reduce arbitrarily or even suppress the sphere in which freedom is legitimately exercised, the result is that the life of society becomes progressively disorganized and goes into decline" (p. 457 § 25). Accordingly, he rejects the totalitarian state on the grounds that it denies man's inherent dignity; the events of 1989 in his mind represent a struggle of moral principles against an "adversary determined not to be bound by moral principles" (p. 456, § 25).

X. Covenant & Polity in Biblical Israel (Daniel J. Elazar)

"A Seminal Work in Biblical Covenant and Polity"

A. The Covenant Idea in the Bible and Politics

1. Introduction

In this well-researched and engaging volume, Daniel J. Elazar, in describing the biblical tradition of covenant, examines the covenantal foundations of Jewish political life, the revival of these foundations in Reformed Protestant Christianity, and the ways that the American polity was founded on this tradition in its "Puritan expression and in its secularized Lockean form" (p. xiii). He defines the covenant as a "morally informed agreement or pact based upon voluntary consent, established by mutual oaths or promises, involving or witnessed by some transcendent higher authority, between peoples or parties having independent status, equal in connection with the purposes of the pact, that provides for joint action or obligation to achieve defined ends ... under conditions of mutual respect, which protect the individual integrities of all the parties to it" (p. 23). A biblical covenant (*"brit"*) "involves a pledge of loyalty beyond that demanded for mutual advantage, actually involving the development of community among the partners to it" (p. 64).

Elazar distinguishes covenants and compacts, which are public in nature, from contracts, which are private. While the former are designed to be perpetual in nature, the latter frequently include terms for abrogation by the parties. A covenant is not like a private legal partnership where each partner has limited obligations to the others; rather it is like "the most comprehensive kind of public law partnership" (p. 69), with extensive mutual obligations.

2. The Bible as a Political Book; the Protestant Reformation

The Bible is an "eminently political book" (p. 60). However, it has not successfully inspired many political orders. After the abortive revolts against Rome in the first centuries of the Common Era, Jewish concern with political matters declined. Christians of the early Church were similarly reluctant in applying biblical principles to the political order; they were instead concerned with individual salvation and were expecting an imminent second coming of Christ.

However, as the centuries passed by, the Bible and biblical ideas of covenant would ultimately find expression in the Protestant Reformation.

Christians would rediscover biblical insights on politics and civic order. In the sixteenth and seventeenth centuries, "the Swiss, the Dutch, the Scots, and the English Puritans not only conceived of civil society in [biblical] covenantal terms, but actually wrote national covenants to which loyal members of the body politic subscribed. Similar covenants were used in the founding of many of the original colonies in British North America" (p. 20). Reformed Protestantism wholeheartedly embraced the covenant concept (p. 26). Based on the idea of sacred covenant, reformed Protestants came to believe that once God establishes a covenant, no human authority can abridge the rights established therein without the consent of the governed.

Especially in Switzerland, a federal theology was articulated (the Latin *foedus* means "covenant"). American constitutionalism merged the concept of covenant with the secularized idea of compact (p. 28).

3. Three Models of Political Society

Elazar describes three systems that have shaped substantial segments of the human race: (i) the covenantal, which tends to be federal; (ii) the conquest based, which tends to be hierarchical and developed through conquest; and (iii) the classical Greek organic system, which tends to be oligarchic and involves "the development of political life from families, tribes, and villages into large polities" (p. 36). The American system, based on the political ideas of the Protestant Puritans, is predominantly covenantal, and thus lends itself well to democracy.

B. The Torah as Ancient Israel's Constitution

The book of Genesis institutes the first covenants between God and man. Elazar calls the Genesis 2 relationship between God and Adam "asymmetrical" and "segmented" (p. 113); the covenant is hence "implicit" (p. 212). Aimless violence follows Adam's disobedience and leads God to the first true covenant between God and man that recognizes man's ability to choose and grants him a formal role in the choosing (p. 113). God thus destroys all life on earth, with the exception of the inhabitants of Noah's ark. The covenant with Abraham is formed in Genesis 15 and 17 and is renewed with Jacob. In Exodus, God establishes a covenant at Sinai, which is reiterated in Leviticus 26. In Numbers 18, God establishes a covenant with Aaron and His House and a covenant in Plains of Moab is established in Deuteronomy 28-30.

While Genesis establishes the first covenants between God and man and the setting for the emergence of Israel and of its constitution, Exodus, Leviticus, and Numbers "constitute the second part based on the exodus from Egypt" (p. 211). In Exodus, the Decalogue is given in the form of two tablets and the Book of Covenant, which enumerates a series of civil and criminal laws, is described (Exo 20-23). In Leviticus, laws and priestly functions and rituals are enumerated. Numbers continues the constitutional corpus and is an indivisible part of the original constitution (p. 184). It discusses the national census by tribes, the divisions of the tribe of Levi and their responsibilities, operational rules for managing the camp, provisions for sacrificial offerings, adjudication of vows, and an allocation for the Levites, among other matters.

Finally, in Deuteronomy, Moses summarizes the history of Israel and puts down all of the laws and revelations he had received in a final form so that they would be memorialized. The book, which ends with the death of Moses, is a "restatement of the entire constitution in a more systematic fashion" (p. 193). The repetition of these laws is especially important to an "oral tradition where repetition is critical to developing recognition if not memorization of texts" (p. 200). While the previous four books served as a constitution for the Jews as a nomadic people, Deuteronomy serves as a constitution that only deals with those laws as applicable to the Jews while living in their land.

C. A Biblical Republic?

1. Joshua

The book of Joshua "describes the classic polity envisaged in the Torah," with the *Eved Adonai* responsible for the civil rule of the *edah* (congregational assembly) and the *Kohen Gadol* responsible for linking the people to God. In Elazar's view, it is "a classic of political thoughts," "a major statement of the class political worldview of the Bible and the regime it advocated," and "the first classic exposition of federal republicanism" (p. 229). The book is divided in an account of the conquests (chaps. 1-12), the division of the land (chaps. 12-21), and Joshua's farewell addresses (chaps. 22-24) (p. 232.). The book explains why the Jews lost or won specific battles and contains instructions to the Jews as to how they should fight. For example, in the case of Jericho, the people were to withhold the desire to loot and personally profit (p. 248). Joshua warns the Jews that they keep God's commandments and, in his words of closing, he warns the people of the consequences that will befall them if they depart from the covenant (Jos 23:14.16).

The book likely emerged during the struggle of Israel against the better armed Philistines. Joshua sought to restore Israel's constitution to its original form in order to reform the confederacy's constitution and better prepare for battle.

2. Judges

The book of Judges was written after the conquest of Canaan in the book of Joshua and before they had a king. Judges contains stories that trace Israel's forsaking of God and His consequent forsaking of Israel. The following cycle repeats throughout the book: (i) the people of Israel begin to worship the foreign gods of the Canaanites that were still living among them; (ii) as judgment for the Jews' following after these foreign gods, God allows the Jews to be conquered by the Canaanites, thus becoming their slaves; (iii) the people of Israel remember God and cry out to Him; and (iv) God raises up a judge (meaning "ruler"), from among them (usually a military leader) who fears God and who helps them conquer their slave masters. Having experienced deliverance from slavery, the Jews live in freedom for a while until they forget God and start to worship false gods once again, thus repeating the cycle.

The book as a whole traces and describes a decline in republican civic virtue. The cycle of backsliding, repentance, and deliverance foresees the redemption of all who repent and turn to Jesus Christ for forgiveness.

D. A Biblical Constitutional Monarchy?

1. General Overview

In Part IV, Elazar deals with the alternate monarchical model of biblical Israel. In the book of Judges, "monarchy is rejected as a form of government consistent with God's covenant" (p. 323). Nevertheless, Saul is made king (p. 330 ff.). Saul's kingship is followed by great tumult as he persecutes David, causing him to go into hiding. In 1 Samuel 21-23, David flees from Saul and hides in the desert. After Saul pursues him, an opportunity arises for David to kill him, but he refuses to do so, for Saul "is the anointed of the Lord" (1Sa 24:7). In this way, David remains faithful to his lord.

The battle with the Amalekites brings about the death of Saul (1Sa 30). When the news reaches him, David weeps and fasts. David is then anointed by the elders of Judah as their king (2Sa 2:4). Meanwhile, the son of Saul, Ishbosheth, is made king of Israel, and war between Israel and Judah follow. David ultimately wins the war (2Sa 4) and becomes king over all Israel (2Sa 5).

2. Government and Covenant in Ancient Israel

Until this point, we have seen God's implicit covenant with Adam, and his explicit covenants with Noah, Abraham, and Moses, and the renewal of the Mosaic covenant under Joshua. In the books of Samuel, God establishes yet another covenant. He says to David: "when your days are fulfilled and you rest with your fathers, I will set up your seed after you, who will come from your body, and I will establish his kingdom. He shall build a house for My name, and I will establish the throne of his kingdom forever" (2Sa 7:12-13). From this "everlasting covenant" (2Sa 23:1-5) comes David's descendent, the Messiah Jesus Christ.

The covenantal governmental framework established by the Israeli Scriptures pursues "a limited but active role in the affairs of society, a role whose level depended upon the needs of the time" (p. 353). It is unclear if from the biblical record the public sphere played a role in education and social services (p. 353). Those principles that animated ancient Israel were theocracy, federalism, and republicanism (p. 354).

3. David as a Precursor to the Christ

In the life of David, we find a window pointing to the Gospel. David's entire life is marked by war and the death of his loved ones, from his "lord" King Saul, to his friend Jonathan, to his first son through Bathsheba and ultimately, the death of his rebellious son Absalom. David experiences firsthand the horrors of sin that have polluted the broken world.

Yet at the same time, David represents a man after God's heart. He is quick to repent of his sins (2Sa 12:13), and his own words at the death of his rebellious and treacherous son Absalom reflect God's own love towards his sinful and rebellious children: "O my son Absalom—my son, my son Absalom—if only I had died in your place!" (2Sa 18:33). We thus find in David's life the mar of sin of even one who is "after the heart of God." His lamentation for his son reminds us of the love of God for all of his children. He would rather take death upon himself than allow that even his rebellious children might perish.

E. Conclusion

I would recommend this book to anyone interested in exploring the idea of covenant in the Bible and how this idea was carried over into America at its founding. In an age where the idea of covenant is being replaced by loose contracts based not on a transcendental view as to the universal good of all of the parties involved, but on the atomistic self-interest of each party divorced from the good of all others and from the good of the community as a whole, this milestone volume is crucial reading.

XI. The Naked Public Square (Richard John Neuhaus)

"A seminal work on church-state relations"

The late Richard John Neuhaus published this seminal work on religion and democracy in 1986 to disprove the myth of a "secular America" that leaves no room for religion or religious values in the public square. Considered by many to be Neuhaus's *magnum opus*, *The Naked Public Square* argues that America's values will not stand when they are divorced from religion.

Contemporary secularists, believing that the Constitution erects a wall of separation between the Church and State, argue that religion must be removed from the American public square in order to respect the intentions of the founders. If such a path of action is undertaken, an "ominous secular silence" will arise whenever we ask by what authority new laws are enacted (p. 248). The removal of religion from American public life will further undermine the absolute truths that have kept society together over the centuries: "The assertion that binds together otherwise different causes is the claim that only a transcendent, a religious, vision can turn this society from certain disaster and toward the fulfillment of its destiny" (p. 79).

Neuhaus argues that the reforms that have been undertaken in America since the war for independence, including the abolition of slavery and the civil rights movement, have been rooted in the religious thinking of leaders such as Martin Luther King, Jr., and Abraham Lincoln, the "foremost theologian of the American experiment" (p. 61). America could not be where it is today, and we would not enjoy the freedoms that we have today, without the inspiration of religion in the public square.

The Naked Public Square, together with the Institute on Religion and Public Life and its ecumenical journal *First Things*, which Neuhaus founded, is a seminal work that has advanced the place of religion in American public life.

XII. A World without Tyranny (Dean C. Curry)

"A notable attempt to articulate a Christian theology of international politics, but one that ultimately fails"

A. Overview

Professor Curry's *A World without Tyranny* is a notable attempt to "articulate a Christian theology of international politics and to relate that theory to the application of Biblical principles in the arena of global politics" (p. xviii). Curry demonstrates his impressive command over international relations as he discusses the political theories and historical movements that dominated the twentieth century and how these movements point to democratic capitalism as the best form of government suited to promoting the common good.

Professor Curry's justification for Christian involvement in the affairs of the world is based on the premise that God created the world and the world was good, yet man tainted every aspect of creation at the fall. God responded through self-sacrificial redemption, and Christians are called to be co-laborers in this redemption by working to establish peace, justice, and order in a broken world.

The book's strength is its impressive outline of a wide array of foreign policy issues, political events, and ideologies that have shaped recent history. Yet ultimately, the book fails in its attempt to define a Christian theology of international politics.

B. Flaws

1. Fails to Clearly Articulate a Biblical Perspective on International Politics

2. Implies that there is No Biblical Perspective on International Politics

Dean Curry's central thesis is muddled by repeated assertions that there is no one "Biblical position" on international politics. The author thus warns against ascribing to the Bible a political agenda. He "does not claim to represent *the* Biblical view of international politics" or to "sanctify partisan positions on specific contemporary foreign policy issues" (p. xviii). Curry contends that the central mission of the Church is to "proclaim that Christ is Lord" and that one of the "greatest dangers facing the Church today comes from those who would replace this mission with a partisan political agenda" (p. 211).

Here, Professor Curry seems to believe that one can extract from the Bible a theology of international politics, yet he warns against deriving from the Bible a "partisan political agenda." The problem with this view is that in adopting the very theology that Curry supports—strengthening America internationally and supporting democratic capitalist systems of government around the world- one cannot escape implicating a political agenda. The idea of strengthening democracies involves a political agenda that is distinct from, for instance, embracing an isolationist policy in international affairs or strengthening socialist governments or international institutions such as the UN. Curry's assertion that there is no Biblical position on international affairs defeats the very purpose of this book.

3. Adopts a Political Agenda despite His Warnings Not to Do So

Despite his warning not to do so, Curry adopts a partisan political positions throughout the book. His argument is that America should support democratic capitalism and oppose other forms of government throughout the world. He writes: "If we take our Christian faith seriously, we will support a powerful United States committed to protecting and enhancing global democracy" (p. 188). The book time and again cites the "superiority of the democratic idea" (p. 59) over other political theories without ever demonstrating in what way the Bible endorses this view or showing how such a view can be adopted without adhering to a political position.

4. Fails to Adequately Support the Thesis that the Biblical Model Supports Democratic Governance

Curry writes that by remaining true to the Church's mission of proclaiming the Gospel, Christians restrain the tyrannical pretensions of human sin and nurture "those values essential to democracy" (p. 211). Yet he fails to show how proclaiming the Gospel nurtures democratic values any more than it does socialist, monarchical, republican, oligarchical, autocratic, or theocratic government. In fact, using the Bible as the only guide, one would never come to the conclusion that democracy is God's preferred form of government. Looking to the Old Testament, theocracy, oligarchy and monarchy were the forms of government of ancient Israel under Moses, the judges and the kings. If we look to the New Testament, socialism more accurately reflects early Church governance than democratic capitalism, for "all who believed were together, and had all

things in common, and sold their possessions and goods, and divided them among all, as anyone had need" (Acts 2:44-45).

The only place we see democracy in the Bible is in the Roman Empire, whose oligarchical republican fusion preserved some democratic elements of ancient Rome. Yet it was this government that sentenced Jesus and his disciples to death and spilled the blood of so many early Christians, thus demonstrating that democracy does not always go hand-in-hand with the human rights and freedom that Curry unyieldingly extols.

5. Failure to Give Any Meaningful Treatment to Christian Separatism

(a) Overview

In his introduction, Professor Curry concedes that for many Christians, the Bible has no place in politics. He writes that "[s]ome American Christians have followed the separatist path of their Anabaptist forebears and shunned any involvement with global politics" (p. xvi). Yet without giving any substantial treatment to the separatist perspective, he goes on to discuss the antithesis to the separatist movement—the view that the "Christian faith demands involvement in the world of international affairs" (p. xvi). Proceeding on the basis that the Bible is profoundly relevant to international politics, Professor Curry argues that in practice, the Christian faith demands influencing their nations' foreign relations in support of democracy through voting, being as well-informed as possible of global affairs and "writing our elected representative and writing letters to the editors of newspapers and magazines" (p. 210).

However, Curry's book is undercut by its failure to address the challenge that separatism poses to his thesis. Besides in the introduction, only the footnotes make a reference to Anabaptists' separatist theology, which he calls "unfaithful to Biblical teaching" (p. 226). This is a shame because the separatist perspective holds a great deal of Scriptural support that Curry's own book is lacking.

(b) The Separatist Challenge

Yet the Bible is ripe with verses that support the Anabaptist position. As Curry himself concedes: "Christ continually reminded those around Him that His Kingdom was not of this world. Tempted by Satan to exercise political dominion over the kingdom of the world, Christ refused" (p. 103). If Jesus had accepted Satan's offer of authority over all of the kingdoms of the world (Luke 4:5-6), He could have immediately taken a position as the functional lord over all of them. While Satan would have remained over him, Jesus could have abolished tyranny and overpowered evil in all societies. Jesus did not give in to the temptation to effect change by participating in the power structures of the kingdoms of the world, and according to Anabaptist theology, neither should those who follow Christ. Rather, Christians should seek Christ's power, which was "not physical or political, [but rather] found in meekness, selflessness, and humility" (p. 103).

In refusing Satan's offer, Christ instead established the kingdom of God, a radical counter-kingdom of love and forgiveness. Anabaptists thus hold that Christians ought to be committed to their citizenship in the kingdom of God, one ruled by the law of love, grace and forgiveness, and shun the domination structures of the kingdoms of the world. Curry writes off this position without giving it any adequate treatment.

6. Adopts an Imprudent Foreign Policy

Curry sets forth a series of foreign policy recommendations based on the imprudent view that democratic capitalism is right for everyone and should be supported everywhere in the world. Chapter 11 sets forth the application of this position in practice. For example, in the Middle East, American foreign policy should embrace "unwavering ... support of Israel" (p. 200) because "Israel is the only democracy governed by the rule of law in the Middle East" (p. 199). In contrast, America should oppose the tyrannies that restrict basic freedoms.

The author fails to concede that many societies fare better off under absolutism than under democracy. This is nowhere clearer than in the Middle East. Where there is democracy in the Middle East, countries are impaired by violence and instability. Consider Libya, which saw the removal of Qaddafi by force and is now ruled by armed militias, or Egypt, which when given the chance to democratically elect its leader, witnessed a *coup d'état* and regular outbursts of violence. Saddam Hussein's dictatorial rule gave to the Iraqi people a level of security and stability that they have not known over the past decade as violence has overtaken democratic Iraq. In contrast, those countries that enjoy stability and security such as Saudi Arabia and Oman are absolutist monarchies that severely restrict freedoms.

Similarly, the author fails to recognize that capitalism may not be a universal model for economic well-being. One need not look further than the East Asian Tigers, some of which in the late 1950s were not much richer than the countries of Sub-Saharan Africa, but transformed their economies through export-led growth without adopting free-market economic policies.

XIII. Creation Regained (Albert M. Wolters)

"Bringing Reformation and Transformation to the Creation"

A. Introduction to the Christian Worldview

In this brief treatise, Albert Wolters develops a Christian worldview that revolves around the three chief themes outlined in the Bible: the creation, the fall, and the redemption. He establishes an ethical system that determines how Christians should respond to basic questions of right and wrong by analyzing moral dilemmas in terms of: (i) how the object of the dilemma was created by God in the original, untainted creation; (ii) how the object fell as a result of man's sin; and (iii) what that object would look like in a redeemed universe.

He begins his thesis in chapter 1 by distinguishing between belief, worldview, philosophy, and theology. While a belief is something that one holds to be true, a worldview colors his entire perception of the world and shapes his decision-making. It involves "our view of the essential nature of humankind" (p. 6). While all people hold a worldview, theology and philosophy are "specialized fields of inquiry that not everyone can engage in" (p. 9). All people, whether they know it or not, hold a worldview; not all hold a philosophical or theological outlook on life.

B. Creation, Fall, Redemption

With this in mind, Wolters sets down a reformational Christian worldview placed "in the broader context of Christian worldviews as a whole" (p. 12). He does this by examining, in this order, creation (chapter 2), fall (chapter 3), and redemption (chapter 4).

In his discussion of creation, he first sets forth a basic distinction between "God's activity of making the world" and the "resulting cosmos" (p. 13), and then shows that these concepts are closely related, since creation is "the correction of the sovereign activity of the Creator and the created order" (p. 14). Wolters distinguishes the laws of nature, which govern the creation, with norms, which govern men's affairs, and then goes on to describe the range of creation, the effects of sin on the fall of creation, and the redemption, which is "cosmic" in that it "restores the whole creation" (p. 69). As a result of the redemption, "marriage should not be avoided by Christians, but sanctified. Emotions should not be repressed, but purified. Sexuality is not simply to be shunned, but redeemed. Politics should not be declared off-limits, but reformed. Art ought not to be pronounced worldly, but claimed for Christ." (p. 71).

C. Structure and Direction

In chapter 5, Wolters distinguishes between *structure*, which is the "'essence' of a creaturely thing," as it was created by God, and *direction*, the "sinful deviation from that structural ordinance and renewed conformity to it in Christ" (p. 88). He discusses the idea of direction as it applies to: (i) the sphere of "reformation" in general; (ii) "societal renewal" at large; and (iii) "personal renewal." Wolters explains that determining the acceptability of certain acts using points of references such as "good" or "bad" are limiting; rather, we should focus on an analysis that takes into consideration the structure and direction of such acts. Nothing in creation is inherently evil or wrong, for "everything created by God is good and is reclaimed by Jesus Christ" (p. 113). The question should be "what is the most effective manner of bringing reformation and transformation to this area of our lives?" (p. 113).

XIV. In the Beginning: Foundations of Creation Theology (Herman Bavinck)

"A Well-Researched Treatise on Creation and Providence"

A. Creation: God as Maker of Heaven and Earth

Herman Bavinck was a Dutch Reformed theologian at the turn of the twentieth century who was heavily influenced by the Dutch minister and politician Abraham Kuyper. In his treatise *In the Beginning*, Bavinck sets out to outline the foundations of a creation theology. He begins by affirming that the story of creation is the "starting point of true religion," because it establishes the distinction between the Creator and the created. This biblical doctrine of *ex nihilo* creation can be contrasted with the religious worldviews of pantheism, which explains the world dynamically, and materialism, which explains the world mechanically and scientifically. Both have the result of blind fate "elevated to the throne of the universe" (p. 56). The Scriptures, in contrast, define the universe as the sum of parts that have been created with their own natures and natural laws and that through their diversity are united to the whole in harmony by a providential Creator. This unity simultaneously serves as evidence of the existence of God. While pantheism and materialism can lead to the deification or the unfathomability of nature, Christianity leads to the glorification of God through the contemplation of nature.

After establishing that the act of creation is attributed exclusively to God in the Scriptures, Bavarck holds that creation is the work of all three persons of the Trinity working in concert to carry out the work of creation. God "created all things through the Son … and through the Spirit" (p 40). For example, we read in John 1:3 with respect to Jesus, the Word, that "all things were made through Him, and without Him nothing was made that was made." With respect to the Holy Spirit, we read in Job 26:13 that "by [God's] Spirit He adorned the heavens; His hand pierced the fleeing serpent."

What was the purpose or goal of this triune creation? Some would argue that the goal of creation is man; the entire universe was created by God for man. Yet Bavinck contends that, because the universe is not "exhausted by its service to humanity, [it] must have some goal other than utility to man" (p. 53). What is this other goal of creation? Scripture declares that it is to proclaim His praise (Ps. 19:1) and to glorify Him (Isa. 43:7). "All kingdoms will be subjected to him and every creature will yield to him" (p. 53). As Tertullian has said, God has created the world "for the embellishment of His majesty" (p. 54).

B. Man's Origins

Chapter 4 of Bavinck's treatise deals with the theme of man as having been created in the image of God. He fleshes out the theory of evolution, points out its inconsistencies, and then brings the reader back to Scripture's story of creation as the only possible true account of the origin of man.

He starts by explaining that the theory of evolution is not new at all. Rather, it had been articulated since the time of the ancient Greeks. In its new articulation, however, humanity is explained *completely* in terms of matter. Bavinck then presents the evidence that has been put forward to support evolutionism and points out that it has from the beginning encountered serious contradictions among scientists and proved completely untenable. Bavinck attacks Darwinism by pointing out that it has been unable to explain both the "origin of life" (p. 143) as well as the "further development of organic entities" (p. 144). Moreover, science has been unable to account for the presence of language, religion, and moral law in humankind, which is completely absent in animals. Furthermore, if Darwin's theory of evolution were true, hundreds of millions of years would be required for man to have reached his present state, but physicists and geologists have objected to these figures (p. 148).

C. Human Nature

In chapter 5, Bavinck brings the reader back to his original idea of the creation of man in God's image, but questions whether this means that man is created in the "image" (archetype) of God or in His "likeness" (a more fluid notion). He gives several perspectives on creation, including naturalism and Roman Catholic supernaturalism, and proceeds to critique each one, finally arriving at the reformation's view of the image, holding that "when man loses that image of God, he does not lose a *substance* and does indeed remain human, but becomes an abnormal, a sick, a spiritually dead human being" (p. 183).

D. Man's Destiny

Man's ultimate destiny is to become like Christ, and thereby gain eternal life. Although Adam was our first ancestor, our destiny does not fully rest on him or on his image, for he was created from the earth and

In the Beginning: Foundations of Creation Theology (Herman Bavinck) 53

was thus dependent on the earth (p. 198). He had not yet realized the full spiritualization of his body. As Adam was the beginning of our race, Christ is the end and final destination.

Bavinck goes on to analyze several questions of pre- and postlapsarian humanity in order to determine which acts were originally forbidden. For example, he states that based on man's dominion mandate over the animal world (Gen 1:28), it must have been that man was permitted to eat meat. The fact that the Scriptures state only that God gave Adam "every herb that yields seed which is on the face of all the earth, and every tree whose fruit yields seed" (Gen 1:29) as food cannot be used to argue that meat was not eaten, since this would be an argument from silence. Furthermore, the sanction in Genesis 9:3 to eat meat ("Every moving thing that lives shall be food for you") should be read not as a new license, but rather, as an affirmation of a previously existing right. It would make no sense that God would only allow the eating of meat *after* the fall; rather, it would seem logical that God would restrict, not augment, postlapsarian rights (p. 211).

Bavinck concludes the chapter with a discussion on traducianism, the doctrine that man's soul is born at the same time of his body, and contrasts it with creationism. While Roman Catholic, Eastern Orthodox, and Reformed theologians generally embraced creationism, Lutherans embraced traducianism because they locate the image of God "solely in a number of moral qualities, in original righteousness" (p. 221). The Catholic and Reformed traditions, in contrast, hold that man's destiny consists in heavenly blessedness and eternal life that he reaches through obedience. The image of God in man may be mutilated through the disobedience of Adam, but by Christ they are "resplendently restored to their destiny" (p. 225).

E. Providence: God's Preservation of the Earth

Bavinck defines God's providence as the "almighty and ever present power of God by which he upholds ... heaven and earth and all creatures and so rules them that ... all things come to us, not by chance but from his fatherly hand" (p. 243). Through providence, God is concerned with every detail of the universe, including the sparrows, the birds of the air, and the lilies of the field. He desires for all to turn towards the good of humanity. Providence involves God's *active will* in ruling *all things*, and in providence is implicit preservation, concurrence, government, and "God's care through the secondary causality of the created order of law as he maintains it" (p. 229). Providence also includes God's speaking, commanding, working, and upholding, as he stands looking on with divine and never passive potency.

Within this framework, secondary causes work alongside providence, the primary cause, to effect change. The secondary causes can be said to be instruments through which the primary cause acts.

Although the Scriptures do not directly use the word "providence," they refer indirectly to it when describing God's creating, renewing, seeing, protecting, preserving, ruling, and His other acts. The word has been used by philosophers and the church fathers to signify foreknowledge, forethought, and, as in the case of St. John of Damascus, as "the solicitude which God has for existing things" (p. 235).

Christian providence must be distinguished from pagan "chance" as well as from the idea of uniformity without variety in pantheism. Deism also mistakenly construes providence as "chance," since the deist god is not concerned with the details of all small things. Socinianism similarly encounters this problem because in opposing the infinite to the finite, God is unable to create the world *ex nihilo*.

Implicit in this idea is providence as divine government. God is a true king because he preserves existent beings and their effects (secondary causes). In Scripture, we accordingly find God described as "King" in the Old Testament and as "King of Kings" and "Lord of Lords" in the New Testament (1 Tim. 6:15; Rev. 19:6).

F. Conclusion

Because of God's providence, Christians should be slow to despair over whatever adversities they encounter in life. God ultimately governs and he is able to turn to our good any and all circumstances that assail us. We must remain patient, steadfast, and faithful, as did His servant Job, and only then receive the fruit of our efforts: a latter blessing that will be greater than the first.

XV. The Last Things (Herman Bavinck)

"Well-Researched, but in Some Ways Flawed"

A. Review

In *The Last Things*, Bavinck brings his readers an ultra-precise exegesis describing the day of Christ's return, man's state between death and resurrection, and the renewal of creation. He divides the book into three parts: (i) The Intermediate State, (ii) The Return of Christ; and (iii) The Consummation.

1. The Intermediate State

In Part 1, Bavinck discusses the question of immortality and the state of humans between death and resurrection. He discusses the state of believers after death according to various Christian perspectives and then presents the Reformed view. Pointing to Scripture drawn mostly from the Old Testament as well as from the Book of Revelation, he asserts that the dead have no knowledge of what happens on earth and cannot intercede for Christians on earth. He compares the veneration of the saints, as well as the veneration of the relics of the saints, as unbiblical.

2. The Return of Christ

In Part 2, *The Return of Christ*, Bavinck, based on science, history, and the Bible, argues that the earth is finite and human history will come to an end. In the end times, the spiritual reign of God will break into history. It will *not*, however, be comprised of a millennial intermezzo followed by a final consummation, as the chiliasts hold. Rather, the Covenant of the Old Testament is in Bavinck's view the intermezzo that will be followed by the "long-aimed-for goal, the direct continuation and the genuine fulfillment, of the Old Testament" (p. 98), the New Testament Covenant through faith in Christ. All believers, whether Jew or Gentile, ought to live their lives as though the Kingdom of God has come and the final return of Christ is coming.

3. The Consummation

In Part 3, *The Consummation*, Bavinck describes the reign of Christ, which will advance until all of creation has been renewed on the day of His return. On that day, the unbelievers will be judged and the believers will be resurrected. This renewal "transforms all matter *(hyle)* into form *(edos)*, all potency into actuality *(potential actus)*, and presents the entire creation before the face of God, brilliant in unfading splendor and blossoming in a springtime of eternal youth" (p. 160).

B. Critique

The tight reasoning and carefully crafted exegeses typical of Bavinck's other works is once again brought to the reader in *The Last Things*. Bavinck claims on numerous occasions that if a particular precept is not in Scripture, then we must not advocate it. Accordingly, Bavinck frequently backs up his theological assertions with a string of scriptural citations.

However, looking up these citations sometimes reveals that they do not directly support the proposition offered. For example, Bavinck states that although God sometimes performs miracles through relics, "they must not be the objects of veneration" (p. 57). He cites Deuteronomy 34:6, 2 Kings 18:4, and 2 Corinthians 5:16 to support his claim. Deuteronomy 34:6 ("the Lord put [Moses] to rest in the valley in the land of Moab opposite Beth-peor: but no man has knowledge of his resting-place to this day") simply states that the location of the relics of Moses are unknown, not that veneration to them would be prohibited had their whereabouts been known. Furthermore, 2 Kings 18:4 ("He had the high places taken away, and the stone pillars broken to bits, and the Asherah cut down; and the brass snake which Moses had made was crushed to powder at his order, because in those days the children of Israel had offerings burned before it") does not speak to the veneration of objects, but rather, to their worship. It reveals God's wrath at those who treat images and objects as gods and offer sacrifices to them. Such a practice must be distinguished from the reverent veneration of objects that were used by God to accomplish His holy purposes, without treating such objects as gods or offering them the worship due to God alone. Finally, the third verse he cites, 2 Corinthians 5:16 ("from this time forward we have knowledge of no man after the flesh: even if we have had knowledge of Christ after the flesh, we have no longer any such knowledge") states that we have no knowledge of man after the flesh, not that the veneration of the relics of holy men is forbidden.

Furthermore, when Bavinck offers scriptural citations that directly support his proposition, such citations are at times taken out of their proper context. For example, Bavinck takes issue with the early Church's practice of making intercessions to the saints, a practice which remains in place in many churches today. He states that such a practice is misguided, since the dead "no longer have a share in anything that happens under the sun" (p. 56). To support this proposition, he cites Ecclesiastes 9:5, 6, and 10 ("the dead are not conscious of anything ... they have no longer a part for ever in anything which is done under the sun ... there is no work, or thought, or knowledge, or wisdom in the place of the dead to which you are going"). Yet these verses cannot be taken literally, for we know from other parts of Scripture that the dead do in fact have thoughts and knowledge. For example, both the rich man and Lazarus knew under what conditions they lived on earth (Luk 16). Similarly, in the final judgment, people will have knowledge of what they did on earth, claiming to Christ that they prophesied in His name (Mat 7:22). Since the Word of God cannot contradict itself, we can conclude that the statements in Ecclesiastes regarding the dead having no thoughts or knowledge are not meant to be taken literally. Rather, these statements must be taken in their hyperbolic context as the cries of a desperate man in an existential struggle for life's meaning.

This causes the reader to inquire: what safeguards are in place to assure that Reformed systematic theology, which interprets Scripture using reason guided by Scripture alone, absent the received teachings of the early universal Church, does not fall prey to the erroneous views of individual interpreters?

www.ingramcontent.com/pod-product-compliance
Lightning Source LLC
Chambersburg PA
CBHW061258040426
42444CB00010B/2414